The Truth About Your Food

Be Smart About

Snack Foods

By Rachael Morlock

Cavendish Square

Published in 2023 by Cavendish Square Publishing, LLC
2544 Clinton Street, Buffalo, NY 14224

Website: cavendishsq.com

Cataloging-in-Publication Data

Names: Morlock, Rachael.
Title: Be Smart About Snack Foods / Rachael Morlock
Description: New York : Cavendish Square, 2023. | Series: The Truth About Your Food| Includes glossary and index.
Identifiers: ISBN 9781502665843 (pbk.) | ISBN 9781502665850 (library bound) | ISBN 9781502665867 (ebook)
Subjects: LCSH: Diet –Juvenile literature. | Nutrition –Juvenile literature. | Snack foods–Juvenile literature.
Classification: LCC TX355 M67 2023 | DDC 641.5/3–dc23

Editor: Rachael Morlock
Copyeditor: Shannon Harts
Designer: Deanna Paternostro

The photographs in this book are used by permission and through the courtesy of: Cover (main) beats1/Shutterstock.com; cover (DNA graphic), back cover, pp. 3, 4, 7, 13, 17, 22-23, 27, 31, 35, 38-39, 42-43, 44-45, 46-47, 48 Omelchenko/Shutterstock.com; p. 5 PR Image Factory/Shutterstock.com; p. 6 Jiri Hera/Shutterstock.com; p. 8 Anthony Berenyi/Shutterstock.com; p. 10 Andrei Metelev/Shutterstock.com; p. 12 wavebreakmedia/Shutterstock.com; p. 14 Kobkit Chamchod/Shutterstock.com; p. 16 Oksana Mizina/Shutterstock.com; p. 18 Ozgur Coskun/Shutterstock.com; p. 20 Maya Kruchankova/Shutterstock.com; p. 23 Sara Carpenter/Shutterstock.com; p. 24 Thongchai S/Shutterstock.com; p. 26 LightField Studios/Shutterstock.com; p. 29 Tyler Olson/Shutterstock.com; p. 30 Thanumporn Thongkongkaew/Shutterstock.com; p. 31 Lilly Trott/Shutterstock.com; p. 34 Olga Miltsova/Shutterstock.com; p. 36 minadezhda/Shutterstock.com; p. 39 SeventyFour/Shutterstock.com; p. 40 Olga Bondarenko/Shutterstock.com.

CPSIA compliance information: Batch #CW23CSQ: For further information, contact Cavendish Square Publishing LLC at 1-877-980-4450.

Printed in the United States of America

Contents

Introduction

Snacking is something most people do every day. It's common for young people ages 9 to 13 to get about 25 percent of their **calories** for the day from snacks, so it's important to be a smart snacker.

Smart snacking focuses on healthy foods. Research shows that the most popular snack foods in the United States are fruit, cookies, chips, ice cream, candy, popcorn, crackers, cake, milk, nuts and seeds, and yogurt. All of these foods can be eaten once in a while, but only a few should be eaten every day. Can you tell which of these foods are the healthiest snacks?

Processed foods like packaged cookies, chips, ice cream, candy, microwave popcorn, and cake have ingredients that can harm your health over time. Whole foods, like fruits, vegetables, whole grain crackers, dairy, nuts, seeds, and eggs, have more beneficial nutrients and can make healthy snacks.

Healthy snacking is about more than just what you snack on. When, why, and how you eat are important too. Snacking too frequently or on unhealthy foods can make it difficult for your body to use all the calories you're taking in.

People snack for a variety of reasons. Most often, snacks are used to satisfy hunger in the time between meals. This is a benefit when snacking keeps you from getting very hungry. Snacking on foods loaded with protein and fiber, or plant material that can help with digestion, can also keep your energy up through an active day.

Try to avoid snacking while doing other activities. Slowing down and appreciating your food can help you listen to your body and enjoy your snack even more.

Snacking is not always a response to hunger, though. Some people snack when they are bored, distracted, or upset. Others snack when they are with friends or at family gatherings because the food is appealing. You can practice mindful snacking by paying attention to what you eat and only snacking when you're hungry.

One way to take charge of when you're snacking is to eat on a schedule. Most kids have a snack before lunch, after school, and in the evening. Planning your snacks in advance makes it easier to have healthy options on hand for times when you know you'll be hungry.

Healthy snacks can be crunchy, creamy, sweet, or salty. They can be convenient too. Whole fruits like apples, bananas, and oranges are easy to pack for a snack. With a little preparation, vegetables can be a tasty and crunchy treat. A handful of nuts can give you the salt you're craving, and plain yogurt topped with berries is both sweet and creamy. There's a whole world of nutritious snacks that can satisfy your hunger and set you up for a healthy future.

Salty potato chips are hard to resist, but a serving of chips won't curb your hunger for long or deliver the nutrients you need. Instead, it's best to only snack on chips every so often.

Chapter One

Processed Snacks

Processed snacks have been sold in increasing numbers since the 1970s. These snacks are manufactured on a large scale in factories. Companies come up with new ingredients that make products taste good, last on the shelf, and inspire shoppers to buy more. Often, this is accomplished by adding lots of salt and sugar to meet buyers' cravings for salty or sweet foods. Even snacks that seem healthy, like breakfast and energy bars, often have high levels of sugar and salt. They might also be made with unhealthy fats and artificial ingredients like food dyes.

Processed snack foods are usually high in calories and low in nutrients. Eating them regularly can impact your health now and in the future. To make healthy choices, it's important to understand how the ingredients in processed snacks affect your body.

Check the Label

You can learn more about the processed snacks you eat by reading the nutrition label. All packaged food in the United States

Nutrition Facts

Serving Size 1/6 package (60g)
Servings Per Container 6

Amount Per Serving	**Mix**	**Prepared**
Calories	260	360
Calories from Fat	80	150
	% Daily Value*	
Total Fat 9g*	**14%**	**26%**
Saturated Fat 3.5g	**18%**	**30%**
Cholesterol 0mg	**0%**	**1%**
Sodium 360mg	**15%**	**20%**
Total Carbohydrate 46g	**15%**	**16%**
Dietary Fiber 1g	**4%**	**4%**
Sugars 28g		
Protein 2g		
Vitamin A	0%	10%
Vitamin C	0%	0%
Calcium	15%	25%

A healthy snack should have about 200 calories and less than 140 grams of sodium. Would the food this label belongs to be a healthy snack?

is required to have a nutrition label that lists the ingredients and includes the amount of various nutrients. The label tells you the daily value for each nutrient based on a diet with 2,000 calories a day. The daily value breaks down the amount of a nutrient by percent. In addition to the daily value, the label also lists a serving size and the number of servings in a package. As an example, a serving of chips may contain 30 percent of your daily value of **sodium**. If there are three servings in a bag and you eat the whole bag, that means you've eaten 90 percent of your recommended sodium for a day.

Sweet Treats

Pure sugar is a natural compound with a very high calorie content. Our bodies turn these calories into energy or store them as fat faster than anything else we consume. Pure table sugar comes from sugar cane, a plant that grows in warm climates like South America. Other natural sugars are honey and maple syrup.

You might have a hard time finding sugar listed as an ingredient in your snack foods, but don't let that fool you. There are more than 200 names for sweeteners in modern snack foods. The list of processed sugars includes high-fructose corn syrup, barley malt, dextrose, modified corn starch, beet sugar, fructose, sucrose, brown rice syrup, malt, sorbitol, invert sugar, fruit juice concentrate, galactose, lactose, polydextrose, turbinado sugar, mannitol, xylitol, and maltodextrin.

High-fructose corn syrup, sometimes called corn sugar, is an artificial sweetener manufactured from corn. It has become so cheap to make that it's now put into snack foods in large quantities. Our bodies digest fructose differently from other sweeteners, and too much of it can affect the liver.

The American Heart Association recommends less than 6 teaspoons of sugar a day for kids and teens, but the average American consumes about 17 teaspoons a day.

High-fructose corn syrup also adds unnecessary calories and weight to our bodies. Rates of **obesity** increased in the United States not long after high-fructose corn syrup was first mass-produced in the 1980s.

Many people eat snacks without realizing how much sugar they contain. The American Heart Association recommends no more than 25 grams (0.88 ounces), or 6 teaspoons, of sugar a day for children and teenagers. Because sugar and sweeteners are found in 80 percent of processed foods, it can be difficult to keep track of all the added sugar in your diet. Just one or two processed snacks can put you over the recommended amount. If you drink a soda every day, you've likely already reached the recommended amount even before having a snack. The average can of soda has 39 grams (1.37 oz), or 10 teaspoons, of sugar.

Salty Snacks

Salt is needed by the body for a variety of different functions. The mineral sodium is present in salt. Sodium plays a role in the body's balance of water and other liquids. It also helps with muscle contraction, heart rhythm, and nerve impulses. The human body cannot manufacture sodium, so we naturally crave foods that contain salt to get what our body needs.

Processed foods are loaded with salt. It's added to improve the taste of snacks or as a **preservative** to make the shelf life longer. Potato chips, corn puffs, corn chips, peanuts, pretzels, salsa, beef jerky, and crackers all have very high sodium content. Many common snack foods that don't seem salty contain sodium, too, such as pudding, doughnuts, chocolate, black licorice, and bagels. High sodium foods have 20 percent or more of your daily value of sodium. In comparison, low sodium foods have 5 percent or less of your daily value.

Our bodies will either use the sodium in salt or dispose of it in our waste. We are not, however, designed to handle excess

Sodium Content	Amount of Sodium per Serving
sodium/salt free	5 milligrams (0.0002 oz) or less
very low sodium	35 milligrams (0.001 oz) or less
low sodium	140 milligrams (0.004 oz) or less
high sodium	400 milligrams (0.01 oz) or more

You can aim for low-sodium snacks using the values on this chart. Grams and milligrams are often used to measure the amounts of things like salt and sugar in foods.

When you cook at home, you can see how much salt you add to food and avoid adding too much. Usually, more than 70 percent of the sodium people eat comes from restaurant food or packaged food.

amounts of sodium. The healthy human body actually needs only about 200 to 500 milligrams (0.007 to 0.02 oz) of sodium daily. It cannot use more than this, and the excess must be removed from the body by the kidneys.

The U.S. Food and Drug Administration (FDA) recommends up to 2,300 milligrams (0.08 oz) of sodium daily for adults. Children need even less sodium than adults. Between the ages of 9 and 13, it's recommended that children take in less than 1,800 milligrams (0.06 oz) of sodium a day. Instead, the

Is Snacking Healthy?

Most young people have between one and three snacks a day. Is snacking a healthy habit? It can be, as long as you're careful about what you eat. Snacking can give you a boost of energy between meals to keep your body powered for all the activities you do in a day.

Snacking can also help you spread out your calories throughout the day. Studies show that breaking up your calories between meals and snacks does not significantly change your **metabolism**. If eating more snacks means eating less at mealtimes, then the act of snacking shouldn't have a negative impact on your health. However, snacking can lead to eating more calories in the day than you normally would. That can cause weight gain.

The other important factor in healthy snacking is choosing healthy foods. Children ages 9 to 13 should eat 1.5 to 2 cups of fruit and 1.5 to 3.5 cups of vegetables a day. Adding produce as snacks can help you meet your fruit and vegetable goals. Snacks high in protein and fiber—such as whole grain crackers with peanut butter, cottage cheese with fruit, or veggies with hummus—deliver the most energy.

average American consumes about 3,400 milligrams (0.12 oz) of sodium a day.

Selling Snacks

Food companies have marketed sweet and salty snack foods to kids for decades. The food and drink industry spends more than $14 billion each year in marketing, and more than 80 percent of that money is used toward advertising processed foods and snacks. However, some changes are being made to help young people snack smarter.

The snacks you typically see in vending machines are processed foods with lots of calories, sugar, and salt.

The Department of Education, which is part of the U.S. federal government, has established guidelines for what can be sold and marketed to kids in schools, including in vending machines. A program called Smart Snacks in School requires that snacks fit in healthy ranges of calories, fat, sugar, and sodium and meet requirements for whole grains. The program only allows schools to sell snack foods with no more than 200 calories per item, less than 200 milligrams (0.007 oz) of sodium, and no more than 35 percent of weight from total sugar.

Some people believe it's important to implement rules such as these to help kids eat healthier foods. Others believe kids should be able to choose what snacks they want to eat at school.

Food for Thought

1. Do you think there should be rules for snack foods in schools?
2. What are some healthy snacks that you enjoy?
3. What kinds of healthy snacks are sold at your school?

Most unhealthy snacks are salty or sweet and hard to resist. However, it's best to think of these snacks as treats and save them to eat on special occasions.

Chapter Two

Daily Health

Many common snack foods, such as potato chips, cookies, cupcakes, doughnuts, pretzels, candy, and ice cream, are not the healthiest snack choices to eat all the time—they're best saved for special treats every so often. They have added sugars, artificial ingredients, or high sodium. They make our bodies work extra hard to process the excess salt and sugar they contain and store the leftover fat. This negatively affects overall health. Having unhealthy snacking habits can put a lot of stress on your body and cause problems even while you're young. If these habits aren't changed, very serious health conditions, like obesity, heart disease, and type 2 diabetes, can develop.

Too Much Sugar

When simple sugars are regularly eaten in large quantities, our bodies cannot keep up. The job of your **pancreas** is to produce a chemical hormone called **insulin**. Insulin is important because it regulates the amount of glucose in your blood. Glucose is a natural sugar that is produced during the digestion process

Packaged yogurt cups are often high in sugar. To cut back on added sweeteners, try topping plain yogurt with fresh or frozen fruits.

and provides the body with energy. Too much glucose keeps blood sugar levels high.

Regularly eating snacks high in sugar causes energy spikes and crashes. While some initial energy will result from eating a sugary snack, it can be followed by a sluggish feeling as the body works overtime to process excess sugar.

Type 2 Diabetes

With the pancreas working harder than ever to produce insulin and break down sugar, a disease called diabetes can develop. Diabetes is a health disorder that results when the body no longer produces or uses enough insulin on its own. When this happens, cells cannot get the energy they need.

The kind of diabetes most commonly found in children is called type 1 diabetes. In type 1, the body doesn't make enough insulin to balance blood sugar. People with type 2 diabetes make insulin, but their bodies don't use it well. Type 2 diabetes is increasing in children ages 10 to 19. According to the Centers for Disease Control and Prevention (CDC), in 2019, about 283,000 children and teenagers had diabetes, and 39,000 of them had type 2 diabetes.

Unlike type 1 diabetes, type 2 can be prevented by practicing a healthy lifestyle. In order to prevent or control diabetes, people often change their eating habits, lose excess weight, and possibly take medications. Monitoring blood sugar levels several times a day is something people with diabetes must do to stay healthy. They sometimes use a sharp needle to draw a small amount of blood. The blood is then tested with a meter to see if glucose levels are acceptable. People living with diabetes can also use a machine called a continuous glucose monitor (CGM) that is worn on the body and measures blood sugar.

Nearly one in ten Americans have diabetes. People with diabetes often regularly check their blood sugar with a device called a glucometer.

Unhealthy Weight

Weight gain can occur when the body converts extra sugar into fat. The human body can only store so much extra fat before it begins to be negatively affected. A person may become overweight or obese. People with obesity have increased risks of high blood pressure, high **cholesterol**, type 2 diabetes, breathing problems, sleep problems, early arthritis (swollen joints), and depression.

About 1 in 6 children and teens (ages 2 to 19) are overweight, and 1 in 5 are obese, according to a survey taken in 2017 and 2018. Childhood obesity has been steadily increasing in the United States. In fact, the rate practically doubled between a survey from 1988 to 1994 and another from 2017 to 2018. The number climbed even higher during the COVID-19 pandemic, and an estimated 22.4 percent of children were obese in 2020. This is a big increase in a short period of time. At least part of the increase is because processed snacks have replaced whole foods in so many people's diets.

The adult obesity rate has been rising too. The CDC says that 41.9 percent of adults were obese in 2020.

Too Much Salt

With too much sodium from salty snacks, your body has to work harder to get rid of the sodium it does not need. Excess sodium builds up in the body, and the body retains more water to compensate for the imbalance. This disturbs the regulation of blood and cell fluids and can result in hypertension.

Hypertension, or high blood pressure, can be a serious condition that causes your heart to pump blood harder and at a higher rate, resulting in damage to the cells lining your arteries. Your veins, muscles, kidneys, and heart all must work

Barriers to Healthy Eating

Obesity is a complex problem. Changing the ways you eat and moving your body more regularly are the best ways to maintain a healthy weight, but that's not as easy as it sounds. There are also factors that are harder to control. The traits a person inherits from their parents, or their genetics, can make them more likely to be obese. Some medications can cause people to gain weight too.

Social factors also put people at risk for obesity. The environment you live in can make it harder or easier for you to make healthy choices. For example, the design of a neighborhood can determine if people have grocery stores or safe places for physical activities where they live.

People with low incomes or limited resources are more likely to snack on processed foods or replace meals with snacks. This is part of food insecurity, or not having enough access to healthy foods. Many people can't afford whole foods. Others only have stores with limited food options where they live. Processed foods are usually cheaper than whole foods, and small amounts can deliver a lot of calories. Individuals can learn how to identify healthy foods on their own, but communities must work together to make whole foods available to everyone.

harder when you eat too much salt. Instances of hypertension in children are rising.

Having an imbalance of sodium in the body on a regular basis upsets the balance of fluids and **electrolytes**. In addition to hypertension, this imbalance can cause diseases and conditions such as the bone disease osteoporosis, heart disease, kidney stones, kidney damage, and sores in the stomach called ulcers.

Many community groups organize food pantries to offer healthy snacks and meals to people who need them.

Other Health Problems

Doctors have seen an increase in kidney stones in young children over the past 20 years. A kidney stone is a hard mass in the kidney, usually formed from calcium. Doctors think the increase is due to salty foods. When too much salt is consumed, the body reacts by producing excess calcium in the urine. Many of the kidney stones in children are probably

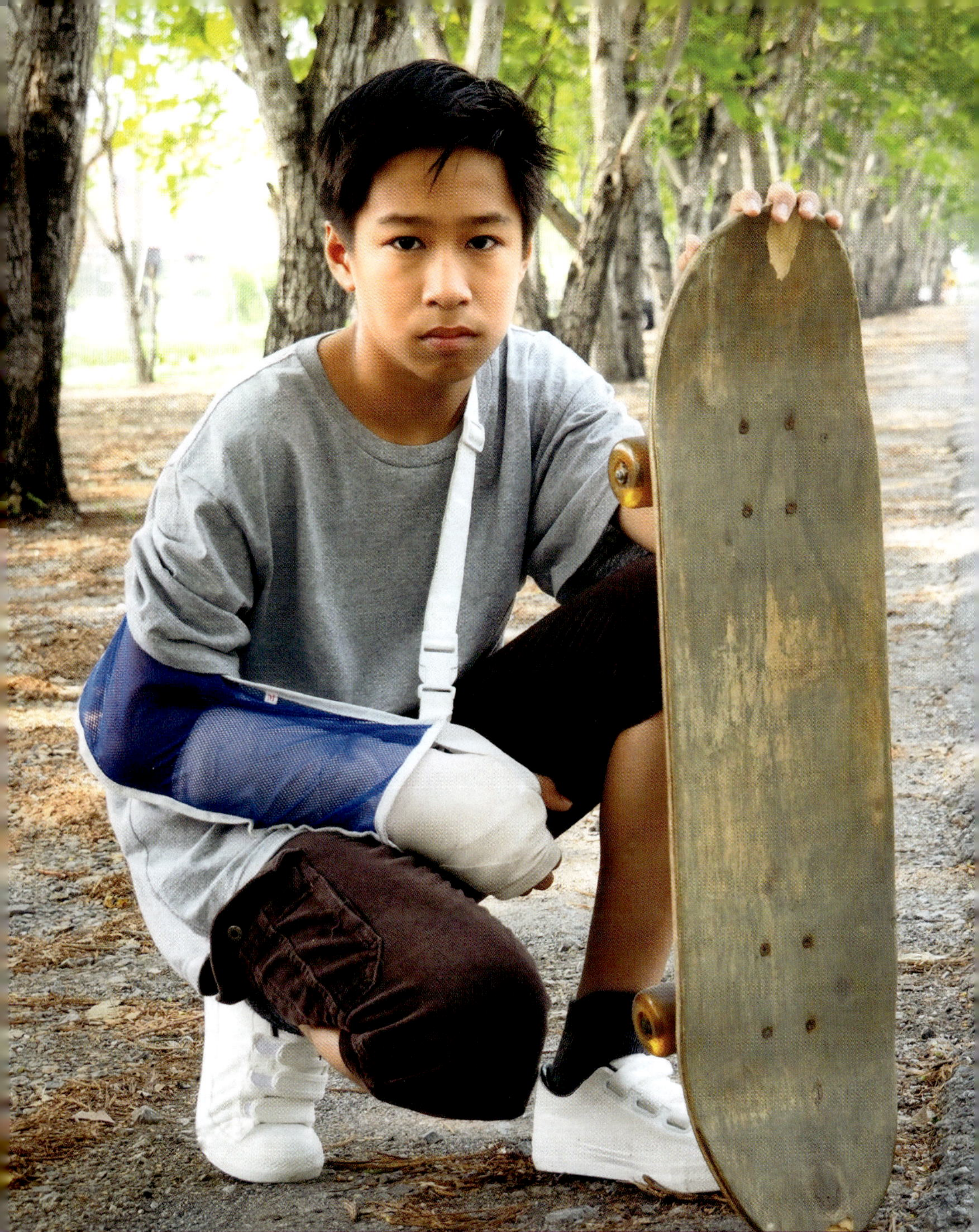

Not eating enough whole foods with the vitamins and minerals you need for a strong body might make you more likely to break a bone.

the result of diets high in sodium from canned, packaged, and fast foods, as well as processed meats.

The combination of high blood pressure, often caused by too much salt, and insulin problems, often caused by too much sugar, makes the body constantly operate in overdrive. Bones and joints become strained from the extra weight, and the body works hard to break down sugars and expel excess sodium, even when resting.

Broken bones among children have increased in recent years as well. Doctors think this is partially because processed foods have replaced more nutritious foods in many children's diets.

Food for Thought

1. How is food insecurity different from hunger?
2. Why are processed foods more affordable than whole foods?
3. Can you think of naturally salty or sweet snacks that can satisfy your cravings without adding processed ingredients?

Many of the factors that cause people to get sick are out of their control. Diet and regular movement are two areas where people can make small changes, like eating more fruits and vegetables whenever possible, in order to improve their health.

Chapter Three

Eating for the Future

Some people can eat processed snacks regularly for years without noticing any health problems. It can be easier for your body to digest sugary or salty foods and burn the excess calories when you're young. Over time, however, eating these foods regularly can harm your health. Too much salt and sugar can cause weight gain, clog arteries, interfere with blood flow, and affect organ functions.

Children who are obese are more likely to be obese as adults. Obesity places people at higher risk of type 2 diabetes and heart disease. In addition, the American Cancer Society has determined that obesity increases your risk of 13 types of **cancer**, including breast, ovarian, stomach, gallbladder, kidney, liver, pancreatic, and colon cancer. Excess fat cells change the level of hormones and proteins in the body, which can make cancer cells grow. Being overweight or obese also increases inflammation, or swelling, in your body and affects your **immune system**. Although eating processed foods increases your chances of developing these serious diseases, eating more fruits and vegetables instead can decrease your risk.

Unhealthy Weight and Diabetes

Too much fat on a person's body causes insulin resistance to increase, and the body has a harder time regulating blood sugar. It's a harmful cycle in which a poor diet causes excess fat and the excess fat affects insulin production.

After years of having diabetes, overworked systems in the body break down. Diabetes can damage nerves in the limbs and can result in numbness and bruising. If left unchecked, reduced blood flow greatly increases the chance for infection to develop. As the limbs are unable to get fuel due to insulin resistance, muscle loss increases. Some people with diabetes eventually need to have their lower legs amputated, but this is uncommon. The eyes can also be affected, resulting in blurred or double vision or even blindness.

Research has shown that diabetes is also linked to the development of heart disease. Higher levels of cholesterol are produced when a person has an unhealthy weight, and this increased fat-like substance in the blood eventually clogs arteries. An insulin-resistant person's body will produce too much insulin in response. The excess insulin causes the liver to produce excess fatty acids. High cholesterol can also cause **gallstones**, which are on the rise for children with an unhealthy weight. Excess sodium in a person's diet adds to this problem too.

Heart Disease

According to the CDC, about 47 percent of adults in the United States have hypertension. People with hypertension

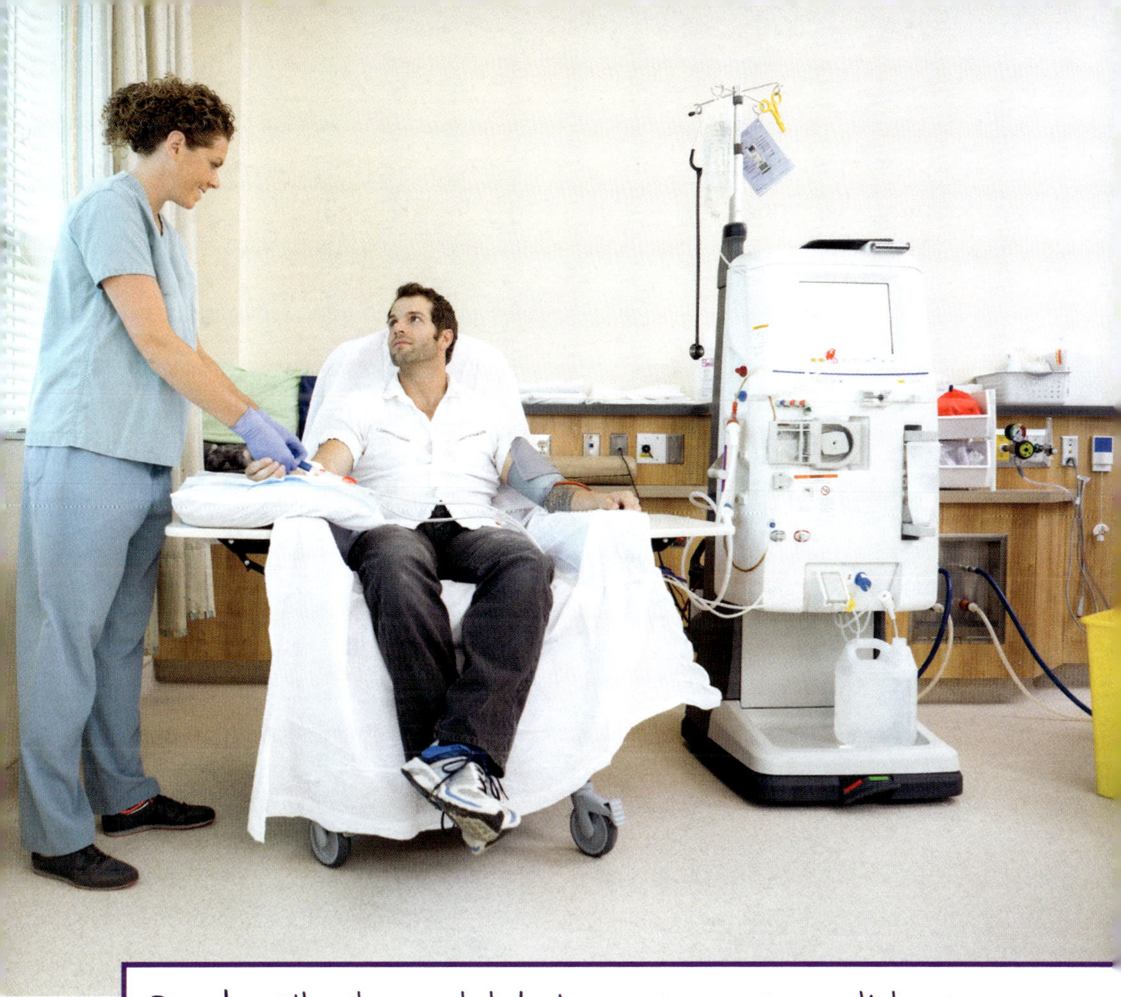

People with advanced diabetes may experience kidney failure and need dialysis treatments several times a week. In dialysis, a person is hooked up to a machine that does the work of the kidneys by filtering waste and **toxins** from their blood.

often need to take medication for the rest of their lives to keep their blood pressure under control. Reducing sodium intake will help lower blood pressure and put less stress on the heart, arteries, and kidneys. Failing to reduce sodium can lead to heart disease.

A heart attack can happen when blood flow to the heart is blocked. In overweight people, the heart is working harder.

When the blood supply that gives energy to the heart muscles is blocked or stopped, a person's heart will stop beating. Depending on the blockage of blood and the length of time the heart stops beating, a person can be killed or disabled by a heart attack.

A blood pressure cuff measures the force of blood pushing against the walls of your arteries as the heart pumps. The CDC considers high blood pressure to be a reading of 130/80 or higher.

Eat the Rainbow

Snacking can be an opportunity to bring more fruits and vegetables into your diet. Fruits and vegetables are packed with vitamins and minerals that can keep diseases at bay. Phytonutrients are substances in plants with special properties that can improve your health. They also give fruits and vegetables distinctive colors. Following the advice to "eat the rainbow," or eat fruits and vegetables with different colors, helps you get a healthy mix of phytonutrients in fresh foods.

Vitamins and phytonutrients act as antioxidants, or substances that positively influence chemical reactions in your body. Antioxidants help your body systems function well and lower your risk of having serious **chronic** diseases—like hypertension, obesity, heart disease, type 2 diabetes, and cancer—in the future. Nutrients from plants can boost your immune system; keep your brain, heart, eyes, and skin in top shape; and even improve your mood.

When you're eating the rainbow, aim for a mix of fruits and vegetables that are red, orange, yellow, green, blue, deep red, purple, white, and brown. Each color group has its own phytonutrients that give it powerful properties. Make sure to wash or scrub fruits and vegetables because you can also often eat the skin. This part of the plant is typically rich in phytonutrients.

Eating the rainbow gives you a range of nutrients. Many fruits and vegetables also have an anti-inflammatory effect. That means they can decrease swelling and keep your body systems running smoothly.

Colorful Fruits and Vegetables

Color	Fruits and Vegetables		Benefits
red	guava pink grapefruit red pepper	tomato watermelon	protect against prostate and breast cancer
orange	carrot mango orange	papaya pumpkin sweet potato	strengthen bones improve vision and eye health boost the immune system
yellow	corn summer squash wax beans	yellow peppers pineapple	prevent blindness and heart disease boost the immune system
green	chard kale spinach broccoli	brussels sprouts green cabbage artichoke kiwi	remove toxins from the body strengthen bones and teeth
blue/ purple/ deep red	berries eggplant plum concord grape	radish beet purple cabbage	maintain a healthy heart support brain function promote healthy aging
brown and white	cauliflower garlic onion mushroom	parsnip banana potato	lower risk of colon cancer control cholesterol levels boost immune system

These examples of fruits and vegetables from the different color groups can help you choose snacks with nutrients that support your health now and in the future.

Discomfort and pain in the chest, shortness of breath, nausea, dizziness, and pain in the arms, back, neck, jaw, or stomach can all be signs of a heart attack. Women may not experience chest pain during a heart attack and may have other symptoms such as upper back pressure and feeling very tired.

Strokes are also related to high blood pressure and diabetes. A stroke is when a blood clot blocks an artery carrying blood to the brain. Having diabetes, an unhealthy weight, and having high blood pressure are all linked to strokes as the body gets older.

Having cancer, diabetes, or heart disease can make a person's life difficult and painful. However, these diseases are less common in parts of the world where people eat fewer sugary and salty snacks. Building healthy eating and movement habits while you're young can help you avoid many of these serious diseases.

Food for Thought

1. Who do you ask for advice or information about healthy food?
2. What motivates you to make healthy food choices?
3. How many different colored fruits and vegetables do you eat a day? What are your favorites?

Adults can chop extra vegetables when they're making dinner. The spare vegetables can make an instant snack.

Chapter Four

Rethinking Snacks

When people hear the word "snack," they may think of quick and easy processed foods they can grab when they're hungry or to satisfy a craving. Chips, candy, and cookies are convenient in the moment, but their ingredients can have a negative effect on your health over time. However, snacking on fruits or vegetables can help you add servings of these important food groups to your diet. Combine a fruit or vegetable with a protein in order to tackle your hunger and pack your snack with energy. The ideal snack should have about 150 to 250 calories, 10 grams of protein, low salt, and no added sugar. You'll find lots of healthy snacking inspiration in cookbooks and on the internet, including social media, that can help you plan snacks that you're excited about eating. Instead of eating the same processed foods repeatedly, healthy snacking can give you a chance to try new foods that nourish your body.

Making Snacks

One way to snack well is to make your own snacks. Sugary and salty packaged snacks, such as sweet breads, cakes, cookies,

When you make banana bread at home, you can let the natural sweetness of the mashed bananas come through instead of loading the recipe with extra sugar.

puddings, pretzels, and popcorn, can all be easily made at home from a few basic ingredients. Making these foods from scratch allows you to control the amount of added sugar and salt. There are also far fewer ingredients than in processed, packaged foods of the same kind.

Making snack foods yourself takes time and is not likely to be something you will do every day. As a result, these snacks will be eaten less frequently or on special occasions. To keep baked goods fresh, make them in advance and freeze or refrigerate them at home. A couple of homemade cookies can be eaten between meals every once in a while as a treat.

Buying Snacks

When choosing store-bought snacks, you need to sift through the ingredients label and look for the serving size, added sugars, and sodium content. If you have a bag of chips in front of you, 11 chips might make up 1 serving. A bag like that can be shared with friends. If you are alone, make sure to put the suggested serving size in a dish and not eat directly from the bag, box, or snack food package. This can keep you from getting too full.

A snack's calorie content is another thing to look for on food labels. On average, children ages 9 to 13 require between 1,400 and 2,600 calories a day. The right amount of calories for an individual depends on their height, weight, age, and activity level. A track runner requires more calories, while someone who has little activity requires fewer. It's important to stay active and balance a healthy diet with activities that will keep your body feeling good and healthy.

The healthiest foods to snack on are fruits, nuts, and vegetables. Celery and carrots are great portable vegetables.

Smart Shopping

Planning ahead is necessary if you want to have healthy snacks available when you're hungry. That means helping your family practice smart shopping at the grocery store. One tip for smart shopping is to mainly fill your cart with items from the perimeter, or outer areas, of the grocery store, instead of from the center aisles.

The perimeter of the grocery store is where most whole foods free from preservatives or added salt and sugar are found. Start in the produce section. If all the produce in your cart is the same color, try swapping out a few items until you have a rainbow of colors. You'll also find meat, dairy, and eggs along the perimeters of the store. Look for snack foods like cottage cheese, plain yogurt, and hummus in the refrigerated sections. You can also find frozen fruits and vegetables that may be less expensive than fresh options.

When you enter the inner aisles of the store, be sure to check the nutrition facts and choose snack foods low in added salt and sugar. Look for nut butters, plain nuts, unsweetened dried fruits, and whole grain crackers.

With some homemade hummus, these can be eaten between meals or when you are on the go. Nuts, such as cashews, walnuts, peanuts, and almonds, have many important nutrients. Remember to buy unsalted nuts whenever possible. Some nuts, such as pistachios, come heavily salted and should only be eaten in small quantities. In addition, honey-roasted nuts that have a coating of added sweetener on them should be enjoyed in moderation.

You can help your family choose healthy options by making a list of whole foods to look for in the store or by being part of the shopping trip.

Small Steps

Making healthy food choices takes practice. It would be difficult to just wake up one morning and have entirely new eating habits. Instead, take small steps to change the way you snack. You might try adding one new fruit or vegetable every week or going with your family to buy produce that's in season from a farmers market.

Plan ahead by packing a healthy snack that's ready to eat as soon as you're hungry.

You can still have your favorite sweet and salty treats once in a while. Just remember that the rest of the time, you can make an effort to eat snacks that have more nutrients you need for growth, strength, and a healthy future. Snacking is often an important piece of the puzzle that is nutrition and healthy living, and making smart snacking choices can be easy and fun!

Food for Thought

1. What might prevent people from swapping processed foods for healthy snacks?
2. How can you help your family focus on whole foods for snacks?
3. What small change can you make today to improve your snacking habits?

Glossary

calorie: A unit of energy that living things get from food.

cancer: A disease caused by the uncontrolled growth of cells in the body.

cholesterol: A fat-like substance found in blood.

chronic: Always present, as in a long-lasting disease or condition.

electrolyte: Any of the ions—from sodium, calcium, and other minerals—in bodily fluids that regulate metabolism.

gallstone: A small, hard mass found in a person's gallbladder.

immune system: The system that protects your body from diseases and infections.

insulin: A hormone made by the pancreas that regulates how much glucose is in the blood.

metabolism: The processes by which a living thing uses food for energy.

obesity: A condition in which too much fat is accumulated and stored in the body.

pancreas: A gland in the body that helps in digestion by producing insulin.

preservative: A chemical added to food products to help them last longer without spoiling.

processed food: A food that has been changed in a substantial way from its original form by adding chemicals, preservatives, and other ingredients.

sodium: A chemical element needed by the body to regulate fluids.

toxin: A poisonous substance.

Find Out More

Books

Martin, Claudia. *Party Food*. New York, NY: Enslow Publishing, 2019.

Peterson, Cris, and David R. Lundquist. *Popcorn Country: The Story of America's Favorite Snack*. Honesdale, PA: Boyds Mills Press, 2019.

Websites

Mayo Clinic
www.mayoclinic.org/healthy-lifestyle/childrens-health/in-depth/nutrition-for-kids/art-20049335
This website from the Mayo Clinic offers in-depth guidelines for the amount of nutrients kids should be eating every day.

Nutrition.gov
www.nutrition.gov/topics/nutrition-life-stage/children/kids-corner
The Kids' Corner page on the U.S. Department of Agriculture's website offers links to interactive websites and games about nutrition for kids.

Whole Kids Foundation
www.wholekidsfoundation.org/assets/documents/better-bites-eat-a-rainbow.pdf
This document from the Whole Kids Foundation provides more information about the phytonutrients in different colored fruits and vegetables and their potential to improve health.

Organizations

American Cancer Society
3380 Chastain Meadows Pkwy NW, Suite 200
Kennesaw, GA 30144
www.cancer.org/
The American Cancer Society is committed to researching and preventing cancer while also providing services and support to people diagnosed with cancer.

American Diabetes Association
2451 Crystal Drive, Suite 900
Arlington, VA, 22202
www.diabetes.org/
The American Diabetes Association aims to prevent diabetes through education, support people diagnosed with diabetes, and work to find a cure.

American Heart Association
7272 Greenville Avenue
Dallas, TX 75231
www.heart.org/
The American Heart Association raises awareness about heart disease, teaches people the signs of heart attack and stroke, and urges prevention of heart disease through healthy lifestyle choices.

Index

About the Author

Rachael Morlock is a freelance writer and copyeditor. She is the author of several nonfiction and picture books for children and enjoys researching new subjects through her work. In the past, she worked as the coordinator of a Community Supported Bakery. Rachael is always interested in supporting local farmers and food producers in Western New York, where she lives with her dog, Rilke.